BE THE AUTHORITY:
How to Write and Publish a Book that Brands You the Authority in Your Field

Ronald Haines

Copyright © 2018 Haines Communications

All rights reserved.

ISBN: 9781726671910

CONTENTS

1   Being an Authority   1

2   Authors are Authorities   5

3   Writing Your Manuscript   9

4   Editing Your Manuscript   13

5   Creating Your Paperback Book   15

6   Creating Your e-Book   21

7   Outsourcing the Work   25

1 BEING AN AUTHORITY

AUTHORITY IN ACTION

Meet small business owners Joe and Sally. Their business has been growing nicely for several years and they are now in a position to start putting money away for retirement. They want to learn about the options available to them, so they go to a business networking meeting where they plan to ask a number financial professionals the same question to see if anyone there seems right for them. They are skeptical about the people in the financial services industry, however, and don't want to deal with any high pressure sales tactics.

They diligently network the room, talk to several financial professionals, but pretty much get the same response from each of them; there is no simple answer to their question so they need to set up an appointment to discuss it further. While this response does appear to make sense, Sally and Joe refuse to set up any appointments. They opt to go home to compare notes about the people they have spoken with, and they leave the meeting carrying over a dozen business cards and without an answer to their question.

The next day they sit down to go through the pile of cards they collected but, unfortunately, they realize that they can't remember much about the individuals they got them from. The cards are all very professional looking and list websites which tout how great each of the professionals are, but to Joe and Sally they all seem indistinguishable.

Now let's imagine that you are a financial professional and the author of a book, and you were also at that meeting. How much better would things have gone for Joe and Sally if, when they asked you their question, you responded with, "I think you'll find the answer you're looking for in chapter 3 of my book," and you handed them a complimentary copy. You shook their hands and parted with a cheerful, non-threatening, "Let me know if I can be of any help."

Having great looking business cards, a well put together website, advanced degrees, certifications, etc. are pretty much the expected norm nowadays for many industries, so none of these things are particularly effective in separating one person from another in the eyes of a prospective customer. What you gave Joe and Sally, however, was the ultimate business card. Instead of pressing for a sales appointment, you provided them with helpful, actionable information while presenting yourself as the authority in your field. When Joe and Sally are ready to set up their retirement account, the chances are very good that you will be the professional that they call.

BECOMING THE AUTHORITY

Whether you are providing a professional service or running any other type of owner-operated business, your business is about you and your personal brand. It, therefore, is essential that you look for ways to stand out against the competition by establishing yourself as the authority in your field. But how, for example, does a health professional such as a dentist or a chiropractor differentiate themselves from other dentists and chiropractors? How can someone in the highly competitive worlds of insurance, real estate or financial services break themselves out of the pack? How does an auto mechanic, a plumber or an electrician let a prospective customer know that their business is best equipped to handle a particular problem? The most common method these professionals generally employ when trying to market themselves is to blow their own horn, but in order to be seen as an authority they need to stop talking about themselves and instead focus on telling what they can do for a prospective client.

Your Credentials Do Not Make You an Authority

While you are justifiably proud of your academic achievements and the letters after your name, your credentials are not going to differentiate you from others in your same profession in the eyes of a consumer. As far as a prospective client is concerned these are simple requirements in order for you to be in that business in the first place. At best your credentials suggest that you may be able to help, but they do not demonstrate that you actually can.

Your Website Is Expected

It may be good news that the Internet has leveled the playing field where even the smallest operator can have a fantastic looking website and an on-line presence rivaling the largest of corporations, but having a website is pretty much the expected norm for any business nowadays.

Plus, the ease with which anyone can be on line has taken us into an age of ever increasing consumer skepticism about what they see on the Internet.

Your Location Is Not Meaningful

It was not long ago that a desirable office address carried a lot of weight in establishing authority, but with virtual office technology anybody can now claim brick-and-mortar space in some of the most prestigious of buildings for less than $100/month, a well-known fact which has considerably diminished the impact of location.

What Makes You an Authority?

Being perceived as the authority begins with providing helpful information to your target audience. That means actionable information in easy to understand English which applies to a prospective client's wants, needs, and challenges. If people recognize that you are the one that can solve their problems you do not have to 'sell' to them, they will come to you ready to buy.

Another way to understand what makes someone an authority is to look at yourself from the prospective customer's perspective. This person doesn't want to hear about you, they want to know if you can resolve their issues for them.

Provided that you are well versed in your business, being branded an authority is not at all difficult. You're an expert in the eyes of anyone who knows less about a subject than you. Everyday things about your business that appear commonplace to you are often revelations to other people, many of whom are eager to learn more. But none of those people are going to jump up and crown you as the authority if the knowledge of what you can do for them remains hidden, so it is up to you to declare that authority for yourself.

Be the Authority

According to Forbes, the number one way to establish yourself as an authority in your field is to write a book, so becoming the author of a book with useful information for your target audience is the ultimate ticket to establishing yourself as an authority. As the author of a book on your selected subject you will instantly be perceived as an expert. Simply put, 'you wrote the book' about it.

Anyone can write a book and get it published, there is no magic involved. If you would like to establish yourself as an expert in your field by becoming the author of your own unique book, simply follow the process presented in this guide and soon you will be the authority.

2 AUTHORS ARE AUTHORITIES

WHY BE AN AUTHOR

While most authors write in hopes of making money from book sales, a frequently cited statistic states that less than 1% of writers ever make more than $1,000 in royalties. With that in mind, you may be asking, "Why then be an author in the first place?" The answer in your case is simple, earning royalties is not the reason you are writing your book. The purpose of your book is to generate clients for your business, and this is going to be accomplished by giving copies of your book away. Once written and published, your per-copy cost of your printed book is not much more than that of a promotional giveaway, so you are easily able to put useful information into the hands of your prospective clients by simply providing them with a complimentary copy.

Of course, once it is published your book will also be available for retail sale, and chances are good you will make some sales, but any royalties you do make should be considered a bonus. In fact, it makes sense to forgo royalties entirely from your e-book version (since there is no cost to you for them anyway) and provide a link on your website where people can download a free copy for themselves. All that matters to you is getting copies of what you have written in front of your prospective clients.

BENEFITS OF BEING AN AUTHOR

Because authors are perceived as experts on the subject they are writing about, being an author gives you instant credibility and dramatically expands the influence of your personal brand. By writing your book you have claimed your authority, and this translates into numerous benefits.

NO MORE OVERT SELLING

Think about the sales process from the perspective of the customer. People do not like a hard sell and are often resistant to setting up a sales appointment or even giving contact information to someone they just met. This hesitation falls away, however, when you are perceived as the expert by a prospective client who knows you wrote a book, even if they haven't read it. Being the author of a book is the perfect ice-breaker and instantly puts you in the role of a consultant rather than that of a salesperson.

BE A SPEAKER

Being an author can give you the opportunity to be a guest speaker at local business functions, service clubs, chamber of commerce lunches and other such gatherings where prospective clients are in attendance. An easy way to accomplish this is to send letters to organizations in your area outlining your presentation (basically, an overview of your book) and offering to give away a couple of copies to attendees via a drawing.

Even if you are not the speaker at a function, make sure you provide a copy of your book as a door prize whenever you go to any gathering where your target audience is also in attendance. Doing so will often give you the opportunity to stand up and make a short plug for your business while announcing to everyone in the room that you are an author.

Media Attention

If you issue a simple news release, or even a tweet on Twitter, about your new book, it is quite likely that the local media will pick up on it.

Getting Your Book into the Hands of Prospects

With the cost of a printed paperback book on par with many promotional giveaways, copies of your book are the perfect items to have at your booth at trade shows. Plus, you'll avoid those attendees who are there to simply collect pens and mugs from the vendors.

If you have a storefront, have copies of your book on the counter for sale. More important than the money you will make from book sales is how impressed your clients will be when they see your book on display. You could also hold monthly drawings for a free copy.

Financial and insurance professionals often buy lists of certain target groups of people, such as those about to turn 65, and send them an invitation to a dinner where they can hear a presentation on a featured topic. These are expensive programs, but the results of a couple of new clients generally more than covers the cost. A more cost effective way to gain clients, though, would be for those professionals to use the mailer to offer prospects a free copy of their book rather than a dinner. This eliminates the people who would come for the free food without any interest in the subject matter, and those who do respond will be real prospects who actually want to read the information in the book.

Someone gives you a lead, but rather than calling them right away to try to gain an appointment you first send a copy of your book with a note saying you received his/her name from ____ and thought that page/chapter ____ may address what it is they are looking for. Chances are good that the prospect may call you before you call them.

There is also a multiplier effect simply by having your books 'out there' because people share will often them with friends, family, and others who have similar needs or interests.

These are just a few examples of the myriad of ways to deliver your book into the hands of a prospective client. As you begin to realize how your book fits so nicely into the marketing strategy for your company you will undoubtedly come up with many more.

You have a unique combination of experience, education and practical knowledge which makes you an expert in your field. You need to write a book in order for potential customers to learn about you and want to seek you out. Many of your competitors will say they can do what you do, but if you're the one who 'wrote the book' on the subject you've demonstrated your authority to a prospective client by showing them your words in print.

3 WRITING YOUR MANUSCRIPT

The first step in creating a book is to write a manuscript which, when finished, will be put through a series of mechanics in order to become an actual book. This first part, the actual writing of the manuscript, is the most time consuming, and for many people the most difficult, part of creating a book. But to be the author of your own unique book, it's going to have to be written in your voice using your words. Fortunately, for the type of book we are going to produce there is a process which makes it very simple.

Your book does have to be lengthy, you're not writing a novel or some detailed business tome. It will be a non-fiction paperback which is specific to the wants and needs or your target audience and written in easy to understand simple English. You're not trying to fill up space or tell a story, the purpose of your book is to get right to the point of delivering useful information. Your book should contain no more than 15,000-20,000 words, so using a rule of thumb that a typical page contains around 200-250 words it will be perhaps 50 to 100 pages long.

Since your book is going to be the solution to a specific need your prospective clients are seeking an answer for, you need to decide whether you are going to write a topic focused book or a target audience focused book before you begin.

Topic Focus

A topic focus book discusses a specific topic within your industry that appeals to a wide audience. An example of this type of book is *Obamacare Explained* (ISBN-13: 978-1484018934), which was published in the year before the major provisions the Affordable Care Act (Obamacare) went into effect. This book explained, in simple English and without any political bias, what was going to happen and gave suggestions about how people could best prepare for it. This was very useful, topical information for a wide variety of people.

Target Audience Focus

A target audience focus book appeals to a specific audience by addressing their unique concerns. An example of this type of book is *I Am Taking Control: Healthy Aging and Financial Security for Baby Boomers* (ISBN-13: 978-1475006001), a book written to address the concerns of Baby Boomers by providing information about how to ensure financial security in retirement. This information is only relevant for the target audience, those people about to turn 65.

If your business serves a wide variety of customer types you may want to select a particular topic to write about, whereas if there is a specific client type you serve then a target audience book makes the most sense. Once you've decided, it is important to stay with that focus rather than try to insert additional information that is not relevant. Your book is intended to provide valuable information which solves a particular problem without adding any fluff. If you come up with several topic ideas or your business has more than one target audience, then write multiple books.

Since your book is to be unique to you, the style, or voice of your book, should be conversational. In other words, write your book as if you were speaking face to face with the reader. Use simple, easily understood words, and avoid jargon whenever possible. If you have to use any terminology that is industry specific make sure to explain what it means.

CONTENT

You know you have a lot of information in your head, but extracting that information and transcribing it into a manuscript can seem like a daunting task. For many people who have thought about writing a book this is probably the reason they haven't done so. But that isn't going to be an issue for the type of book you are writing.

Get started by making a simple list of the most common questions that your clients and potential customers ask you about. Then make another list of the things that people should know but probably don't know to ask about.

Next, pull together all of your promotional materials, sales letters and blogs you have written, and anything else you are currently using to promote your business and your brand. Go through this and copy anything that pertains to the two lists you have made.

What you are now going to do is take each question from the two lists and write out an answer in about 1,000 words. You probably have some of this done already in the promotional material you have gathered. You should be able to write the answers to these questions in about an hour for each, so if you make the commitment to writing one answer per day you can have the writing part of this project completed within 2-3 weeks. Each one of these can then be a chapter in your manuscript, although similar questions can easily be combined into a single chapter. When you're finished you should end up with 12 - 15 chapters.

Remember that none of what you have written to this point is going to be about you; the main content of your book must be about providing useful information to the reader. The final chapter, *About the Author*, is where you will talk about yourself and your credentials. Once the reader has read your book and has already concluded that you are an authority, this chapter lets them know where your expertise comes from and serves to validate their opinion of you.

In addition to the chapters you have written, you will also need to add a Title Page, a Copyright Page and a Table of Contents. These will usually be added to the manuscript during formatting.

Organization

I recommend using a word processing program for writing your manuscript, making each question a separate file. However, programs like Microsoft Word can become a bit unwieldy when you find yourself juggling up to 20 such files, especially when it comes to compiling it all into a single manuscript later. An excellent way to keep yourself organized while writing and then being able to easily pull it all together is to use a program called Scrivener. Many writers use Scrivener, and it is highly recommend that you buy a copy and spend a few hours learning the basics of how it works before you begin your writing.

Once you have your manuscript written the hard part is over, the rest of the process is just mechanics and details. Set your work aside for a couple of days, then come back to it to read it carefully and correct any errors you can find. You manuscript will then be ready to move on to the editing phase.

4 EDITING YOUR MANUSCRIPT

Having your manuscript written is exciting and it is natural to want to rush to getting your book into print, but it is very important to have any errors that you missed in your document corrected and you make sure that you have the text exactly the way you want it to be seen in print before you proceed. This is done in editing, a procedure which should not be skipped.

Editing is the process to check your manuscript for grammar and spelling errors and, if necessary, re-word for better flow. Since you wrote your manuscript you are too close to it to be an effective editor. So, while it is entirely your choice whether or not to hire a professional editor, it is highly recommended that it be someone other than you who does your editing.

There are three different levels of editing, a line edit (around $7.50/page), a copy edit (around $4/page), and proofreading (around $3/page).

LINE EDITING

A line editor performs a creative edit and will check for writing style and language use, but this level of editing is not needed for the type of manuscript you have written so you shouldn't have to pay top dollar for your edit.

Copy Editing

A copy editor performs a mechanical edit and this is the preferred edit for you book. A copy editor will check for:

- Punctuation errors
- Spelling errors
- Grammatical errors
- Typographical errors and inconsistencies
- Errors in consistency and appropriateness of verb usage

Proofreading

A proofreader will go over your manuscript and correct punctuation, spelling and grammatical errors, but will not perform an in depth a job as a copy editor.

Depending on the type of editing you have done, the cost for having your manuscript edited will run from a low around $150 to a high of about $800. If the cost of editing is a concern, at least have someone else go over your manuscript before you move on to the next step. A low (or no) cost alternative to a professional edit could be to have a couple of friends or family members do this for you.

Once your manuscript has been edited and you are satisfied with it, your document is then ready to be formatted.

5 CREATING YOUR PAPERBACK BOOK

The next step is to convert your manuscript into an actual book and get it published as an industry standard, 6x9 trade paperback with a color cover. Rather than using a traditional publisher, the easiest and quickest way to accomplish this is to self-publish with KDP, Amazon's Print-On-Demand technology. Using KDP enables you to maintain creative control over your book, you will own the copyright, and the ability to print on demand means your book will never be out of stock. Print on demand also means that there is no minimum order, so you can order as few or as many copies as you want at a time.

Using KDP is also extremely cost effective in that you are able to purchase copies of your paperback book at Amazon's cost of only $2.15 per copy (at the time of this printing). With the suggested retail price exceeding $15 per copy, your printed book becomes an affordable yet very effective, high-impact promotional giveaway.

If you are proficient with word processing programs like Microsoft Word you may be able to format your book yourself, but the easiest way to get it formatted is to use a template. Templates are readily available for download, just do a search for 'book template' on-line and select one for a 6x9 book. KDP also provides some free resources you may wish to use.

When you create your file using a template, be sure to remove all of the existing template information such as guides, template layers, and filler text to keep this from appearing in the final print.

Page Numbering

The pages in your book will have to be numbered and each chapter should begin on an odd numbered page, so you may have to insert blank pages as you go along. All pages, including the blank pages, should be numbered sequentially with even numbers on left pages and odd numbers on the right. Using templates simplifies this tremendously since your template will number the pages automatically.

Trim Size

Trim size is simply the size of your published book. Trim size measurements are listed as width by height, so the trim size of your 6x9 paperback means the printed book will be six inches wide by nine inches high.

Margins

Margins are the blank sections of a page that wrap around your printed content. They prevent your manuscript text from getting cut off at the edges.

The inside margins are called Gutter Margins. This is the blank space on the inside edges nearest to the book binding that prevents your manuscript text from extending into the binding. The minimum required gutter margin is based on the number of pages in your manuscript, essentially the thickness of your book. A template will take care of this for you, but if you are not using a template KDP will let you know the size of the gutter margins you will need to use.

The blank spaces at the top, bottom, and outside edges that prevents your manuscript text from getting cut off during printing are called Outside Margins.

The section of the page inside the margins is called the Safe Zone.

BLEED

Bleed is the term for printed objects that you want to extend completely to the edge of a page, such as images, backgrounds, and graphics. Objects meant to bleed are required to extend beyond the final page size so that when the page is trimmed, there won't be any white edges. Since your book will not be including these types of objects you can just select 'no bleed' when KDP gives you that option.

Prior to publishing your file must be converted to a PDF (Portable Document Format), but you can upload your manuscript using a standard word processing file such as DOC or DOCX, which is standard with most templates, and KDP will automatically convert these file types into a PDF for you. The only exception here is if your book is to contain borderless images that you need to bleed, in which case you would have to convert your document to a PDF yourself prior to uploading it.

ISBN

ISBN stands for International Standard Book Number, which is a unique 10– or 13-digit number assigned to a published book and shown both on the copyright page and on the back cover. An ISBN identifies a book's edition, publisher, and physical properties. You have the option to purchase your own ISBN through one of the internationally licensed distributors, or else KDP will provide you with one at no cost. Bowker is where you would purchase one from in the US for a price of $125 ($150 with a barcode), or you can get discounts if you purchase ISBNs in bundles of 10 or more.

The advantage to purchasing your own ISBN is that you could then sell the rights to your book and retain the ISBN, whereas if you used a KDP assigned number you could not move it and would have to have your book re-published. However, since the purpose of your book is to position you as the authority in your field and not to become a best-seller in hopes of being picked up by a major publisher, using the free ISBN from KDP works well for your purpose. The publisher is not listed as KDP but as Independently Published when using their free ISBN.

Cover Design

You will need two images for your book cover, one being an appropriate image for the front page (actually, a cover image is not required so this is optional), and the other an image of yourself for your back cover. The front cover image can be one you provide yourself or you can download one from a site called Pixabay, which offers a wide variety of free images under the Creative Commons license. Since Pixabay does not provide model release documentation, however, I would suggest only using images from them where no person is clearly identifiable.

For optimal printing, all images should be at least 300 DPI (Dots per Inch). Images less than 300 DPI will be flagged prior to publishing and you will be asked to resubmit either a new one or an updated one.

As with the inside of your book, you can elect to design your own cover or use one of the many cover templates available online. KDP's free program called Cover Creator offers several templates to select from, and you will probably find one of them to be more than adequate.

Since your book will be less than 100 pages, you do not have to worry about putting wording on the spine of the cover since the book will not be thick enough.

The back cover will include your author image, book description, and the ISBN with a bar code. If you used KDP's free ISBN the Cover Creator program will automatically generate the bar code for you.

Proofing

After you submit your formatted manuscript and cover to KDP an on-line book proof is generated and submitted to you for review. This is where you will be glad you had your book properly edited because any changes you make at this point can affect the layout of all of the pages after that. The KDP previewer shows exactly how your book will look in print so be sure to check every page, especially checking for any spacing errors. If you do find errors simply fix them on your formatted manuscript and then re-submit it.

When you are happy with the proof you simply click to approve it and KDP will then review your book. If they find any errors you will be notified by email and provided with details about how to fix them. Once past the KDP review, your book will usually be available for print-on-demand publication within 48 hours.

ROYALTIES

While the primary purpose of your book is for you to purchase copies for your marketing efforts, you can have your book listed for sale in the various Amazon marketplaces and also make your book available to bookstores and other on-line retailers through Amazon's expanded distribution channel. This is simply a matter of setting a retail price for your book and clicking the appropriate boxes. Depending upon the selling price you designate, you can earn royalties from these retail book sales. For books sold through the Amazon marketplaces your royalties will be 60% the list price you set minus the printing costs. Sales through the expanded distribution channel earn 40% minus the printing costs.

The printing cost is all you pay for the author copies that you order for yourself, which is currently $2.15 per book.

RONALD HAINES

6. CREATING YOUR E-BOOK

Books nowadays come in two versions, print and electronic, but the formatting that worked for a paperback will not work for an e-book and vice versa. With your printed book, you've taken the time to provide the best reading experience you can for your readers and your paperback looks great because of your efforts in making the text fit into each carefully numbered page. An e-book, however, cannot have such a static format because it needs to be able to flow. The people reading your e-book can be doing so using a variety of different devices, such as e-readers or smart phones, so the text must be formatted in a way that it can wrap and resize automatically as readers zoom in or out. Also, page numbers need to be removed since the pages need to reformat themselves to fit the screen of the device they is being viewed on. In addition, the table of contents needs to be made clickable so the reader can jump directly to a particular chapter. This is all accomplished by converting your manuscript into either a MOBI file for Amazon Kindle, an EPB file for other e-book retailers such as Barnes & Noble and Apple iBooks, or both.

To prepare your manuscript for conversion to an electronic file you first need to remove the earlier formatting, which is most easily done by copying your manuscript and then re-pasting it into another word file as plain text (make sure to keep your original). More information about this can be obtained for free at Smashwords; they refer to this procedure as the nuclear option. Then, as with the print book formatting, there are a number of e-book templates available for you to download, many of them free, to drop your clean text into to create a version of your manuscript that is ready for electronic file conversion.

File Conversion

E-books can be produced and made available on platforms such as Smashwords, Draft2Digital and Amazon Kindle, each of which will convert your manuscript to the appropriate electronic file and provide an ISBN for free. You cannot use the ISBN from your paperback because each version of your book is required to have its own unique number, so make sure you delete it from your copyright page when preparing your e-book manuscript.

E-books made available for sale on these platforms can also be published on other platforms and sold through any number of other retailers without restriction. Smashwords and Draft2Digital are open publishing aggregators which make it easy for you to gain exposure to a wide buying audience because these platforms have large distribution channels (including Barnes & Noble, iBooks, Kobo, Scribd, and many more) which you can place your e-book with.

For those authors who agree to publish only on Kindle, Amazon offers a program called KDPS (Kindle Direct Publishing Select) where in exchange for exclusivity Amazon offers promotional tools such as free e-book days, countdown deals, Amazon Ads, and inclusion in Amazon's KU (Kindle Unlimited) program, which is an e-book subscription service.

If you do not wish to participate in the Amazon's KDPS program you don't need to convert using Kindle if you use Draft2Digital because they offer Kindle as an option in their distribution channel and will make the appropriate conversion for you.

Cover Design

You will need to create a new cover for your e-book, but this cover is much simpler than the one you made for your paperback, and in most cases you can use the same cover image. There are a variety of ready-to-use templates available, including the free Kindle Cover Creator, so creating a cover for your e-book is quite simple.

PRICING AND ROYALTIES

As with your physical book, depending upon the retail price you select for your e-book you may earn royalties here also. You also have the option to have your e-book listed for free (except for Amazon which requires a minimum price of 99 cents) and then provide a link to the free e-book on your website, in your emails, or in any of your other marketing material.

RONALD HAINES

7 OUTSOURCING THE WORK

While this guide has provided you with all of the tools needed to produce your books yourself, you may feel that you don't have the time to write your own manuscript or that the mechanics of book creation isn't something that you wish to deal with. You still want to be the author of your own unique book, however, so rather than letting these potential stumbling blocks prevent you from becoming that author you can simply outsource those parts that you do not wish to do yourself. It's quite easy to hire other people for any of the steps necessary to create your book, and depending upon your budget you can even elect to outsource the entire project. Listed below is a guide to what you might pay for each of the component pieces, should you choose to not do them on your own.

GHOSTWRITING

The most effective book for establishing your authority will be in your voice and written in a conversational style, but it is possible to achieve this without writing it yourself by having your manuscript ghostwritten. Busy business professionals are often unable to devote the time required to do the actual writing, so as a result many business books nowadays are ghostwritten. A ghostwriter will interview you to obtain the source material and capture your voice, and will then write your manuscript for you and deliver it in a timely manner. When you hire a ghostwriter you will own the manuscript and you will still be credited as the author.

While using the services of a ghostwriter may be a very efficient way to get your manuscript written, it can also be a rather costly option. Ghostwriters typically charge either by the page or the word and rates are in the range of:

Per page: $75 - $175

Per word: $.25 - $3.00

So for a 50 page/12,500 word manuscript you will be looking at a minimum cost of about $3,125, and most likely a lot more. Considering the cost involved, it often makes sense to first hire a ghostwriter for a trial chapter, around 2,500 to 3,000 words, to decide if you like their style before contracting with them to produce the complete manuscript.

Ghostwriting is simply that, the actual production of your manuscript. The document will still need to be edited and formatted before it can be converted into a book.

PAPERBACK AND E-BOOK MECHANICS

There are many professional services listed on Google, but a good place to look for someone to handle your book mechanics is on a site called Fiverr, where before you hire someone you can read reviews about their work. The prices listed below represent the approximate averages you will find on Fiverr.

EDITING

As mentioned earlier, the cost for having your manuscript edited will run from a low around $150 to a high of about $800. Keep in mind that an editor's function is to put the final tweaks on a finished manuscript; they will not re-write it for you if it is poorly prepared. If your manuscript is not ready for editing and you are unable to properly prepare it yourself you may want to consider hiring a ghostwriter to finish it for you.

Paperback Formatting

Expect to pay from $200 to around $1,000 to have someone format your print manuscript.

Paperback Cover Design

Fiverr lists many people who will create your paperback book cover for you in the range of $15 to $45.

E-Book Formatting

You can have your e-book formatted for as low as $15 to a high of around $100.

E-Book Cover

As with paperback book covers, Fiverr lists many people who will also create your e-book cover. Expect to pay in the range of $10 to $40.

The Bottom Line

Outsourcing your book falls into two broad categories, the creative part of preparing the manuscript and the mechanical part of editing, formatting and cover creation. An average cost to have the entire process done for you would be around $5,000, but if you shop around you could probably bring that down to $4,000 or less.

Clearly, the biggest cost in outsourcing your book is having it ghostwritten, but if you write your own manuscript you could then turn the mechanical parts over to others and have your book formatted and published in both paperback and electronic versions for as little as around $500

ABOUT THE AUTHOR

Prior to creating Haines Communications, Ronald Haines, a many-times published author of both non-fiction and fiction books, spent over 25 years running a health insurance brokerage helping small businesses and sole-proprietors. During this time he wrote two books for his business, both of which established him as an authority in highly competitive marketplaces.

The first of these books was published in 2012. With many of his clients approaching retirement age, Ronald decided to expand his brokerage business to include indexed annuities and Medicare supplements. To enable him to stand out in the competitive arena of financial services he wrote *I Am Taking Control: Healthy Aging and Financial Security for Baby Boomers*, which advises people approaching retirement to challenge conventional wisdom and personally take control of their future. By establishing himself as an authority he was able to sell these new products to his existing health insurance clients, and he credited his book with bringing his brokerage many new clients as well.

On March 23, 2010, the Affordable Care Act, the most sweeping piece of social legislation to be passed since Medicare and Medicaid in 1965, was signed into law and went on to be known as Obamacare. Many of the provisions were quietly implemented during the following three years, but the biggest impact which would change the face of health insurance in America forever took effect on January 1st, 2014. Realizing the effect this would have on his clients and other small business owners, Ronald wrote and published a book called *Obamacare Explained* in order to get the word out to them about what they should be doing in 2013 in order to preserve the type of health insurance they currently had and also to save their businesses considerable money before the final piece of Obamacare occurred. *Obamacare Explained* became a best seller on Amazon as both a paperback and an e-book, but the biggest impact was not in the royalties that Ronald earned. It was the number of invitations to speak at various business organizations and the calls he received from business owners asking him to meet with them that made 2013 a banner sales year. *Obamacare Explained* had instantly made Ronald an authority in the highly competitive field of health insurance. Even other insurance agents were buying his book.

Ronald Haines is currently the president of Haines Communications, a book writing and publishing service offering a complete writing and publication package for less than the cost of ghostwriting alone.